Original title:
Cuddle Up in Dreamy Land

Copyright © 2024 Creative Arts Management OÜ
All rights reserved.

Author: Natalia Harrington
ISBN HARDBACK: 978-9916-90-388-9
ISBN PAPERBACK: 978-9916-90-389-6

### The Garden of Dreaming Souls

In quiet corners where shadows play,
Petals of hope in the light of day.
Whispers of wishes ride on the breeze,
Dancing among the swaying trees.

Each flower tells tales of joy and strife,
Cultivating dreams, nourishing life.
As sunbeams glance off dewdrops bright,
This sacred space feels just right.

## Hushed Nighttime Murmurs

Stars twinkle softly in velvet skies,
Moonlight wraps secrets in gentle sighs.
A lullaby sings to the sleeping earth,
In shadows, the night breathes a quiet mirth.

Crickets converse in melodic tones,
While the world slips into dreams unknown.
Each moment is stitched with silken thread,
As whispers of night weave tales unsaid.

## A Haven for Wandering Minds

In a realm where thoughts can roam free,
Every idea is like a leaf on a tree.
Branches extend into worlds untold,
With stories of warmth and echoes of old.

A path of imagination, winding and bright,
Illuminated softly by twinkling light.
Here, hearts can flourish, and passions ignite,
In this haven of dreams, everything feels right.

## **Softened Whispers of Tomorrow**

Hope tiptoes softly on morning dew,
A promise of change painted in hue.
Each dawn feels tender, a fresh start anew,
With dreams like flowers, in gardens they grew.

In gentle sighs, the future awakes,
As the sun climbs high, the shadow breaks.
With every heartbeat, a chance to embrace,
The whispers of tomorrow, a warm, bright space.

## **Enchanted Slumber**

In a realm where dreams take flight,
Moonlit whispers paint the night.
Stars weave tales of long ago,
In slumber's arms, we softly go.

Waves of peace, a gentle tide,
Where shadowed secrets often hide.
Close your eyes, let worries cease,
In this haven, find your peace.

## Cosmic Naptime

Underneath the twinkling sky,
Galaxies drift and softly sigh.
Each star a lullaby that sings,
Embracing us with borrowed wings.

Planets spin in dreams so deep,
While stardust weaves a silent sweep.
Close your eyes and float away,
To where the cosmos softly play.

## Embrace of the Silken Cloud

A cloud of silk in twilight's glow,
Carries whispers, soft and slow.
Wrapped in warmth, the world drifts by,
In this space, we breathe and sigh.

Gentle breezes lift us high,
Past the worries, past the sigh.
Floating dreams, a tranquil sea,
In the silence, we are free.

## **Harmony in Hibernation**

Beneath a blanket, warm and still,
Nature rests, her heart does fill.
Silent whispers, soft and low,
In hibernation, time does flow.

Gentle rhythms, pulse of peace,
In the quiet, worries cease.
Dreams like snowflakes gently fall,
In harmony, we hear the call.

## **Driftwood Dreams and Twinkling Skies**

Beneath the waves, the driftwood lies,
Whispers of time in starlit skies.
Each fragment tells a tale so deep,
Of currents' grace and secrets to keep.

A soft breeze brushes the moonlit shore,
Carrying dreams of those who explore.
With every tide, new stories arise,
Beneath the glow of twinkling skies.

## Embracing the Shadows of the Mind

In corners dark where secrets hide,
Shadows dance with nowhere to bide.
Embracing fears with tender grace,
Finding strength in a silent space.

Thoughts like whispers, gentle and clear,
Guide us through what we hold dear.
Beneath the weight, we learn to find,
Light that blooms in the mind's own kind.

## **Sleepy Wishes in a Starry Nest**

Cradled soft in dreams' embrace,
Wishes drift in cosmic space.
Twinkling stars weave tales of night,
A lullaby in silver light.

From sleepy hearts, our hopes take flight,
Guided by the gentle night.
In a nest where dreams entwine,
Sleepy wishes soft, divine.

## Echoes of Peace in a Dreamy Vale

In a vale where shadows play,
Echoes of peace softly sway.
Whispers of nature's sweet refrain,
Carried by the gentle rain.

Mountains stand with timeless grace,
Guardians of this tranquil space.
In every breeze, a sigh released,
Harmony, our hearts' greatest feast.

## **Lullabies Beneath the Cotton Clouds**

Whispers dance on the gentle breeze,
Cotton clouds float with such grace.
Stars twinkle in twilight's embrace,
Soft melodies drift through the trees.

Crickets sing in a soft refrain,
The world slows down to a calm.
Moonlight bathes the fields in charm,
Nature's rhythm eases the strain.

Sweet dreams cradle the sleeping earth,
As shadows whisper their goodbye.
In this hush, wonder starts to fly,
To a realm of unmeasured worth.

Close your eyes, let worries fade,
Beneath the sky painted in blues.
A symphony of hope renews,
In lullabies softly laid.

## A Hug of Dusk and Dawn

Twilight wraps the earth in gold,
The sun whispers secrets to the night.
Stars peek out, shy and bold,
A canvas of dreams in fading light.

Branches sway to a gentle tune,
The air thick with a sweet scent.
Magic dances as day is spent,
A promise lingers beneath the moon.

In the quiet, shadows merge,
Colors blend in soft delight.
Daybreak waits, ready to surge,
Bringing warmth to the soft midnight.

Embrace the cycle, the sweet interlude,
Where dusk and dawn intertwine.
Life's moments, effortlessly align,
In the hug of time, feel renewed.

## The Embrace of Night's Gentle Breath

In the hush of the starry expanse,
Night wraps softly around the earth.
With every heartbeat, dreams advance,
Awakening magic, love, and mirth.

Moonbeams, silver threads of grace,
Weave through shadows, peaceful and light.
In this quiet, we find our place,
Holding whispers of the night so bright.

Crickets play their tender song,
As the world rests, embraced in peace.
It's where all hearts naturally belong,
Under night's gentle, sweet release.

Breathe deeply of the darkened air,
Let worries drift far, far away.
In the stillness, find your prayer,
In night's embrace, forever stay.

## Serene Moments on a Cloudy Pillow

Gray skies blanket the waking world,
Soft whispers linger in the air.
Clouds like pillows gently unfurled,
Cradle dreams without a care.

Raindrops tap on the window's glass,
Nature's rhythm, a soothing sound.
In this moment, calmness will pass,
As peace and solace can be found.

Time slows down in the muted light,
Every worry fades like a dream.
Clouds offer shelter, soft and slight,
Boundless serenity flows like a stream.

Nestle deep in comforting thoughts,
In the embrace of the cloudy sky.
Here in stillness, joy is sought,
Moments of calm, drifting high.

## **Fantasies Wrapped in Velvet Dreams**

Soft whispers weave in twilight's glow,
Mysteries dance where shadows flow.
A world of wonder, calm and deep,
In velvet dreams, our secrets keep.

Through shimmering lights, our spirits soar,
With every heartbeat, we explore.
In the folds of night, we're forever free,
Fantasies bloom, like wildflowers, we see.

## **Slumber's Sweet Serenade**

Gentle sighs in the evening hush,
Crickets chirp in a soothing rush.
Moonlight drapes on the world's sweet face,
In slumber's arms, we find our place.

A lullaby sang by the stars above,
Whispers of peace, a tender love.
In dreams, we wander, hand in hand,
In slumber's hold, we understand.

## **Cocooned in the Tapestry of Night**

Threads of silence in darkness weave,
A quiet world where we believe.
Wrapped in shadows, soft and near,
Cocooned in night, devoid of fear.

The sky unfolds its starlit quilt,
In every corner, magic's built.
Together we drift on whispers light,
Bound in the tapestry of night.

## **Warmth Beneath a Blanket of Stars**

In the cool embrace of the evening's sigh,
We lay beneath the vast, endless sky.
Stars twinkle like dreams waiting to start,
Wrapped in a warmth that melts the heart.

Every shimmer a wish, a hope to hold,
Stories of love, endlessly told.
Cocooned in wonder, nature's art,
We find our place, together, apart.

## **Midnight's Embrace**

Stars flicker in the night,
Dreams take flight in silence,
A gentle breeze whispers,
Wrapping the world in calm.

Moonlight paints the trees,
Casting shadows long and deep,
The world drifts into slumber,
Held close in midnight's arms.

Time stands still in darkness,
Where secrets softly breathe,
Each sigh a lullaby,
Cradled in night's embrace.

## Clouds of Soft Whispers

Gentle clouds drift above,
Carrying secrets of the day,
A symphony of soft sounds,
Whispered dreams float away.

Beneath their tender shrouds,
The earth sighs with relief,
Nature hums a sweet tune,
Wrapped in soft disbelief.

Sunlight peeks through layers,
Painting shadows on the ground,
Each moment a fleeting breath,
In the hush that wraps around.

## **Cradled in Cosmic Silence**

Under the vast night sky,
Stars twinkle like lost hopes,
A silence that speaks volumes,
In the dark, the heart copes.

Galaxies swirl in stillness,
Creating paths of stardust,
Whispered wonders beckon near,
In the quiet, we find trust.

Time bends in cosmic dance,
Each heartbeat a gentle sigh,
Cradled in the void's embrace,
With dreams that dare to fly.

## Enveloped in Softness

Morning breaks with a hush,
Soft light spills across the land,
Each blade of grass awakens,
Touched by a gentle hand.

Petals open to greet day,
Colors glow with pure delight,
Nature bathes in warm embrace,
Enveloped in soft light.

The air carries sweet fragrance,
A symphony of life sings,
In this realm of tender peace,
Joy in every moment clings.

**Pillows of Serenity**

In quiet rooms, the whispers flow,
Soft fabrics cradle thoughts, aglow.
The world fades into gentle sighs,
As peace unfolds beneath the skies.

Beneath the stars, our dreams take flight,
Embracing shadows, chasing light.
A haven found in textures warm,
Where hearts are safe from any storm.

## **Moonlit Reveries**

The silver beams weave tales of old,
In night's embrace, the secrets told.
Whispers dance on a velvet breeze,
As time stands still, our minds at ease.

Reflections glow on the river's face,
Carrying dreams to a distant place.
In soft luminescence, we drift away,
Painting the night with colors of gray.

## **Feathers in the Night**

Softly falling, the whispers glide,
Caressing moments we cannot hide.
Like feathers drifting from above,
Whispers of peace, and whispers of love.

With every breath, the night unfolds,
A tapestry of stories told.
In gentle hues of dusky dark,
We find the light, the quiet spark.

## **Velvet Dreams Awaken**

In velvet realms where dreams reside,
We journey deep, where hopes abide.
A touch of magic in every seam,
Awakening hearts, igniting dreams.

As dawn approaches, shadows flee,
Our spirits rise, wild and free.
Wrapped in warmth, the day begins,
With softest light, our souls it wins.

## The Calm Before Wakefulness

In the hush of night's embrace,
Dreams linger in a soft trace.
Whispers float on gentle air,
Moments held with tender care.

Stars blink softly in the skies,
As the world in silence lies.
A breath held, a heart so still,
Awaiting dawn's sweet, warm thrill.

Shadows dance with quiet grace,
As the night begins to chase.
Every thought starts to unwind,
Leaving peace for dawn to find.

In the calm, a promise waits,
As the sun hesitates.
In this pause, life takes a breath,
Embracing light, defying death.

## Serene Visions in Twilight

As the sun dips low and sighs,
Painted hues embrace the skies.
Gentle breezes brush the trees,
And the world finds tranquil ease.

Whispers of the evening calls,
Bright reflections on the walls.
Colors blend in soft embrace,
Nature wears a velvet face.

Footsteps fade on winding paths,
Echoes of the daylight's laughs.
Underneath a glowing dome,
Heart and spirit find their home.

In the twilight's tranquil glow,
Peaceful streams of thought will flow.
Wrapped in dusk's embracing shroud,
Silent dreams will speak aloud.

## **Explorers of Gentle Horizons**

Wandering where the skies meet sea,
Adventurers brave, wild and free.
Chasing shadows, tracing light,
Finding paths in day and night.

Softly drifting on the breeze,
Carried forth with utmost ease.
Limitless where hearts can soar,
Each horizon opens more.

Sunlit trails and starlit streams,
Filling life with vibrant dreams.
Echoes of the world they roam,
Every land becomes their home.

Together, hand in hand they share,
A journey steeped in love and care.
With every wave and breath they take,
Explorers of the dawn will wake.

## **Secrets of the Midnight Hour**

In the quiet of the night,
Secrets whisper to the slight.
Moonlight spills like silver dew,
Revealing paths both old and new.

Hidden dreams and silent fears,
Unravel tales wash down like tears.
Each heartbeat echoes like a chime,
In the stillness, steals the time.

Thoughts emerge like ghostly sighs,
In the dark, the spirit flies.
Underneath the starry veil,
Life's true stories tell the tale.

Midnight holds a mystic power,
Gifting wisdom in the hour.
In those moments, deep and wise,
The truth appears, divinely ties.

## The Quilt of Tranquil Whispers

In the hush of night, soft whispers play,
Stitching dreams in twilight's gentle sway.
Threads of silver pull the moonlight low,
Each secret shared begins to softly glow.

A tapestry of thoughts, delicate and bright,
Woven with love, in the deep velvet night.
Silent promises in starlit weaves,
Lay the heart open, as the spirit believes.

Every fold a memory, every seam a song,
In the quilt of whispers, where our souls belong.
Gentle breaths of peace wrap around,
As tranquility's essence quietly resounds.

Embrace this quilt, let the worries cease,
In the warmth of night, find your sweet release.
For in each stitch lies a tranquil kiss,
A reminder of the world wrapped in bliss.

## **Hibernation in the Garden of Stars**

In a garden where celestial lamps shine,
Stars bloom softly, in silence divine.
Nature whispers as the world takes rest,
Wrapped in dreams, under night's gentle crest.

Each petal a secret, each leaf a sigh,
Colors mix softly, beneath the sky.
Cocooned in stillness, the heart beats slow,
As whispers of stardust begin to flow.

Hibernation calls from the depths of the night,
Cradled in shadows, until morning light.
A symphony of silence, a sweet serenade,
In the garden of stars, where dreams are laid.

So close your eyes, let the world just drift,
In this dreamy haven, find your gift.
With the stillness of time and the night's soft glance,
Let the stars cradle you into their dance.

## Seraphic Sojourns in Dreamland's Glade

In the heart of silence, where dreams converge,
Seraphs dance lightly, on whispers they surge.
Beneath the moonlight, where shadows play,
Journey to realms where the spirit can sway.

Glimmers of wonder in each gentle sigh,
Awakening fantasies that softly lie.
With every heartbeat, let your spirit glide,
Through shimmering paths on the starry tide.

Nestled in solace, where echoes resign,
The glade unfolds magic, pure and divine.
A world untouched by the hands of time,
In dreamland's embrace, all souls climb.

So wander through dreams, let your heart soar,
In seraphic sojourns, find what you adore.
For in the glade, where wonders unfurl,
Every whisper is gold, in this enchanted world.

## Twilight's Embrace of Whimsical Starlight

As twilight descends, a canvas unfolds,
A dance of starlight, in hues of gold.
Whimsical shadows play, twirl, and weave,
In the gentle embrace that no one will leave.

Stars whisper secrets to the darkened skies,
Painting the heavens with soft lullabies.
Each twinkling shimmer, a dream taking flight,
In the arms of twilight, everything's right.

The world slows down in this magical hour,
Bathed in the glow of a celestial flower.
With each breath taken, peace starts to bloom,
In twilight's embrace, there's always room.

So let go of worries, let your spirit ignite,
In the whimsical starlight that dances at night.
For in this embrace, all hearts intertwine,
Held close by the wonders of the divine.

## **Whispers of a Twilight Embrace**

Gentle winds through trees do sway,
Casting shadows, night meets day.
In the hush, soft voices call,
Echoes linger, love enthralls.

Stars aprowl in velvet skies,
Bringing dreams where beauty lies.
Hearts entwined in silent tune,
Underneath the rising moon.

Whispers dance like fireflies bright,
Lighting paths in tender night.
Guiding souls, they softly weave,
In the twilight, we believe.

Time stands still, we feel the glow,
In each moment, peace will flow.
Embraced by night, we find our place,
Lost together in this space.

## **Moonlit Comforts of the Soul**

By the shore, the waters gleam,
Moon's reflection, like a dream.
Softly waves whisper a tune,
Cradled close beneath the moon.

Night unfolds its tranquil grace,
Stars aligned, a warm embrace.
In the stillness, hearts align,
Wrapped in love's celestial sign.

Breath of night, so cool and sweet,
Carrying the rhythms' beat.
With each heartbeat, time suspends,
In the darkness, joy transcends.

Dreams take flight on silver beams,
Unraveled threads of whispered themes.
In the quiet, we find our part,
Moonlit comforts warm the heart.

## **The Nest of Starlit Sighs**

In the boughs where silence thrives,
Nestled close, are starlit sighs.
Comfort found in whispered night,
Wrapped in dreams, the world feels right.

Delicate as lace, a dream,
Floating gently on moonbeams' gleam.
In each breath, the calm arrives,
In the nest of starlit sighs.

Listen close to nature's breath,
Life entwined, defying death.
Hope and dreams, they softly blend,
In this space, we find our mend.

Every star, a memory's glow,
Guiding where our hearts may go.
In this nest, we rest our eyes,
Cradled in the starlit skies.

## Soft Horizons in Slumber's Hold

Gentle hues of dawn arise,
Whispers soft as morning sighs.
Cradled dreams of night unfold,
Painting skies in shades of gold.

In the stillness, time stands still,
Calm descends, a tranquil thrill.
Clouds like pillows gather near,
Casting shadows, sweet and clear.

Slumber's hold a tender guide,
Carrying hearts, where dreams abide.
Each horizon glows anew,
Promising a world so true.

As we rest, the day will break,
In soft light, our hopes awake.
Together, we will greet the dawn,
With open arms, life moves on.

## **Radiance of Soft Places**

In the glow of dawn's embrace,
Fields of gold begin to grace.
Whispers dance on gentle air,
Beauty blooms with tender care.

Petals soft, like dreams they sway,
Fleeting joys that softly play.
Sunlight kisses every hue,
Painting life in colors true.

Every corner holds a spark,
In the silence, love leaves its mark.
Here, the heart finds sweetest rest,
In soft places, feeling blessed.

## Slumbering Under Glimmering Lights

Stars above in velvet skies,
Softly wink with secret sighs.
Moonlight wraps the world in peace,
As dreams begin, and worries cease.

Whispers float on evening's breath,
Carrying tales that dance with death.
Each glimmer tells a story old,
In silent hours, the night unfolds.

Lullabies beneath the glow,
Nature's magic starts to flow.
In slumber's hold, the heart takes flight,
Chasing dreams beyond the night.

## **Shadows of Peaceful Moments**

In twilight's hush, the shadows blend,
Carrying tales that never end.
Moments lost, yet held so tight,
In the stillness, hearts take flight.

Gentle echoes of the past,
Crafting memories that will last.
Softly woven, threads entwined,
In peaceful shadows, love is blind.

Every sigh a whispered prayer,
Floating softly on cool night air.
In the quiet, solace grows,
In shadows deep, the spirit knows.

## **Hushed Tides of Imagination**

Waves that lap on distant shores,
Carry tales and secrets, ours.
In the hush, ideas glide,
Through currents deep, they sway and ride.

Starlit skies, a canvas wide,
Where dreams and thoughts are free to bide.
In the quiet, visions bloom,
Filling every silent room.

Tides of hope and whispers blend,
In this realm, where thoughts transcend.
Hushed moments, softly play,
Imagination leads the way.

## **Echoes of Moonbeams in Cozy Corners**

In the silence, whispers dwell,
Captured secrets softly tell,
Moonbeams dance on floors so bare,
Echoes linger in the air.

Shadows stretch and gently play,
Guiding thoughts that drift away,
In each corner, dreams ignite,
Cradled in the arms of night.

Softly glows the silver light,
Bathing hearts in restful sight,
Where the world feels far and wide,
In this charm, we can abide.

Every sigh a story spins,
Wrapped in warmth where hope begins,
Echoes cradle every heart,
In these corners, love won't part.

## A Sanctuary of Echoed Dreams

In the stillness, thoughts unfold,
A sanctuary, safe and bold,
Whispers weave through dusk's embrace,
Echoed dreams find their place.

Hidden corners, secrets flow,
In this haven, soft and slow,
Memories wrapped in gentle light,
Embrace the stillness of the night.

Softly sighs the velvet air,
Nurtured in the warmth we share,
Hope and longing intertwine,
In this space, our spirits shine.

Every heartbeat softly sings,
In the calm, true comfort clings,
Here in dreams, our souls align,
Together in this sacred shrine.

## The Cocooned Realm of Softest Light

Wrapped in warmth, a gentle pull,
The cocooned realm, serene and full,
Softest light begins to glow,
Cradling all we wish to know.

In the shadows, whispers creep,
Hidden promises to keep,
Here, the heart finds peace to rest,
In this realm, we are the blessed.

Woven tales in silken seams,
Living quietly in our dreams,
Every moment feels so right,
In this cocoon of tender light.

As the world outside may fade,
In this space, we aren't afraid,
Love and hope in silence grow,
In the softness, we will flow.

# **Wandering the Woven Dreams of Evening**

As the sun dips low and fades,
Wandering through twilight glades,
Woven dreams in colors blend,
As the evening whispers, send.

Each step taken, softly free,
Lost in thoughts, just you and me,
Through the pathways made of starlight,
We explore the charms of night.

Echoes of laughter fill the air,
Moments cherished, beyond compare,
In the twilight's gentle grasp,
Time feels like a warm, sweet clasp.

With every breath, our spirits soar,
Wandering where the heart does roar,
In these dreams, we find our place,
Ever woven in love's embrace.

## **Dreams Dance on Feathered Winds**

Whispers float through twilight skies,
Carried forth on gentle sighs.
Colorful dreams take airy flight,
Chasing shadows into the night.

Feathers brush against the moon,
Swinging to an ancient tune.
Hopeful hearts on breezes glide,
Where fantasies and wishes bide.

In this realm where wishes play,
Every moment feels like May.
Sparkling visions weave and swirl,
In the dreamscape, magic twirls.

Glide on wings of pure delight,
Dance till dawn, embrace the light.
For in dreams, we find our grace,
Floating softly, a timeless space.

## Starlight's Gentle Kiss

Under the veil of cosmic sights,
Whispers thread through endless nights.
Each star a wink, a knowing glance,
Inviting hearts to dream and dance.

Moonbeams weave a silver lace,
Embracing all in soft embrace.
In starlight's glow, we find our way,
Guided gently to break of day.

Moments tremble with pure bliss,
In the silence, a lover's kiss.
Wrapped in warmth of twinkling gleams,
We drift upon the edge of dreams.

Time stands still in the night's caress,
Each heartbeat echoes, a sweet confess.
For in this glow, worries cease,
Wrapped in starlight's gentle peace.

## **The Warmth of Forgotten Tales**

Pages worn with time's embrace,
Stories linger, memories trace.
Voices echo through the years,
Filling hearts with joy and tears.

Beneath the dust of ancient lore,
Dreams and hopes reside once more.
Rivers of time gracefully flow,
Carrying tales we've come to know.

In shadows cast by flickering light,
Laughter dances in the night.
Whispers weave through the air so sweet,
As every tale finds its heartbeat.

Gather near, let memories reign,
In the warmth, we feel no pain.
Each story shared, a cherished gift,
In the bond, our spirits lift.

## Nurtured by Night's Quiet Charm

Crickets sing a lullaby,
Underneath the velvet sky.
Gentle breezes softly sway,
Wrapping dreams in twilight's play.

Stars emerge, a diamond show,
Lighting paths where shadows go.
In this hush, our thoughts take flight,
Dancing softly in the night.

Moonlight drapes a silver sheen,
Painting visions, sweet and serene.
In the dark, new stories grow,
Nurtured gently, hearts aglow.

Let the night embrace your fears,
Hold them close, release the tears.
In its charm, find solace deep,
As dreams awaken from their sleep.

## **A Gentle Tidal Caress**

Waves whisper softly on the shore,
Carrying secrets from afar.
Moonlight glistens like silver ore,
Cradled beneath a twilight star.

Sand flows like laughter in the breeze,
Footprints left in a fleeting dance.
Oceans echo tales to the trees,
In this tranquil, timeless expanse.

Seashells nestled, treasures hide,
Nature's gifts brought by the tide.
Each pulse, a promise, gentle guide,
In the stillness, dreams abide.

With every swell, a serenade,
Hearts adrift in a soothing place.
In the water's arms, hopes are laid,
A gentle, tidal, warm embrace.

## **Dancing Among the Stars**

In the velvet of the night sky,
Stars twinkle like dreams set free.
Galaxies swirl, as if to sigh,
Whispers of worlds we long to see.

Constellations weave tales above,
Guiding souls on journeys vast.
In their glow, we feel the love,
Of stardust paths woven in the past.

Each flicker sparks a restless heart,
As we sway to cosmic tunes.
With every twirl, we play our part,
Under the glow of silver moons.

In this grand ballet, we find grace,
Gliding through the infinite night.
In the universe's warm embrace,
Our spirits soar in pure delight.

## **Resting Under Celestial Canopies**

Beneath the vast, embracing skies,
We lay upon soft, grassy beds.
With every sigh, the world replies,
As day melts into night's cool threads.

Clouds drift like thoughts, serene and slow,
Painting stories with every hue.
In the twilight, dreams begin to grow,
A tapestry of hope anew.

The stars emerge, a bright parade,
Filling hearts with ancient lore.
In their glow, our worries fade,
As we breathe the cosmic core.

Time pauses here, under the spell,
Of celestial wonders, vast and grand.
In silence, every heartbeat tells,
Of love that binds, of dreams once planned.

## **Warmth Beneath the Stars**

A fire crackles, sparks take flight,
Casting shadows on our dreams.
Beneath the stars, our hearts alight,
In the glow, we find our themes.

Stories spoken in the night,
Wrapped in laughter, wrapped in sighs.
Each moment dances, pure delight,
Underneath these endless skies.

The cosmos watches, silent friend,
As whispers weave throughout the air.
In this space, our hearts extend,
To share the burdens we must bear.

With every star, a wish we send,
The warmth of love, a guiding light.
Together, let time gently bend,
As we embrace this perfect night.

## **Effervescent Echoes of Whimsy**

In a garden of dreams, colors collide,
Laughter dances, no need to hide.
Whispers of joy float on the breeze,
Tickling hearts, putting minds at ease.

Bubbles of wonder rise to the sky,
Chasing the clouds, oh so spry.
Joyous moments twirl in the air,
Embracing the light, without a care.

Each fleeting glance, a playful stroke,
The canvas of life, where hope awoke.
In every giggle, in every shout,
The essence of whimsy lingers about.

So let imagination's colors run free,
Painting the world, just you and me.
In this realm where laughter stays,
We'll weave our dreams in whimsical ways.

## Hibernating in a Blanket of Stars

Under the night sky, softly we lay,
Endless warmth in starlit display.
Crickets serenade, a gentle song,
Wrapped in silence, we belong.

Dreams woven like threads of silver light,
Journeying far, beyond the night.
With every twinkle, secrets unfold,
Whispers of magic, forever told.

The moon watches over, a beacon so bright,
Guiding our hearts through the soft twilight.
In this stillness, our souls ignite,
Hibernating together, hearts take flight.

As we drift deeper into the serene,
Amongst the echoes of what's unseen.
Cradled by night in a soft, sweet hold,
We become part of the cosmos, bold.

## Enveloping Warmth of Night

As the sun dips low, shadows embrace,
Night unfurls in a velvet grace.
Cloaked in twilight, the world softly sighs,
Whispers of dreams float towards the skies.

The stars emerge, glimmering bright,
Guiding lost souls through the night.
Wrapped in peace, the silence sings,
Cradled by moonlight, our spirit springs.

In this haven, worries take flight,
Bathed in the glow of soft, warm light.
Comfort surrounds like a gentle tide,
In the arms of the night, we confide.

So let the hours drift slow and serene,
Beneath the sky's vast, starry sheen.
In the warmth of the dark, we find our place,
Together, in this tender space.

## **Tender Threads of Tranquility**

In a garden of peace, our hearts entwine,
Soft whispers dance, a sacred sign.
Beneath the boughs, where shadows lie,
We weave our dreams, just you and I.

The gentle breeze carries sweet refrain,
Tales of solace in the falling rain.
Nature's lullaby, a soothing stream,
Cradling us softly, like a dream.

Sands of time slip soft and slow,
Flowing like rivers in a tranquil glow.
In every heartbeat, calmness reigns,
Uniting our souls, erasing all chains.

Here in this moment, we softly tread,
With tender threads, all fears shed.
Entwined forever, in harmony found,
In this tranquil space, our love is crowned.

## **Hibernation of the Heart**

Winter whispers soft and low,
The heart finds peace in the snow.
Silent dreams linger and sway,
As time slows down, night becomes day.

Wrapped in shadows, warmth resides,
In tucked-away worlds where love hides.
Frosty breath on window panes,
Hope remains as the cold wanes.

Under the stars, stories sleep,
In quietude, secrets we keep.
Awaiting spring's gentle restart,
The world will bloom, and so will the heart.

## Connecting Through Soft Spaces

In whispers shared, our spirits dance,
Through quiet moments, love finds chance.
Gentle touches bridge the divide,
Where hearts unfold, and dreams reside.

Eyes meeting in a timeless gaze,
We linger longer in this haze.
Soft laughter echoes, light and free,
In sacred spaces, just you and me.

The world fades out, it's just us two,
In the hush, all feels brand new.
With every breath, we draw in light,
In these soft spaces, we ignite.

## **Illuminated by the Night's Glow**

Under a canopy of stars so bright,
The moon whispers secrets in silver light.
Shadows dance, weaving tales untold,
Night's embrace is warm and bold.

Starlit paths guide wandering souls,
To hidden dreams and distant goals.
In the stillness, hearts intertwine,
Illuminated by the night's design.

Every flicker tells a story deep,
Of love and loss, of promises we keep.
With each heartbeat, the universe flows,
Forever changed by the night's glow.

## **The Tranquil Nest**

In the heart of the quiet woods,
Soft feathers cradle dreams,
Sunlight filters through the leaves,
Nature's gentle lullabies seam.

A nest holds stories untold,
Swaddled in warmth and peace,
The chirps of life unfold,
As all worries find release.

Branches sway with soothing grace,
Whispers dance upon the air,
In this sacred, cozy place,
Time is still; nothing compares.

Embrace the calm, let it nest,
Within the arms of serene days,
This tranquil haven, our best,
A cradle of nature's ways.

**Muffled Echoes of Comfort**

In twilight's embrace, shadows play,
Soft sighs dance upon the breeze,
Echoes linger, gently sway,
Muffled tones put our hearts at ease.

Familiar laughter fills the air,
Wrapped in warmth of old refrain,
Through the cracks, love's moments flare,
Timeless memories, free from pain.

Gentle whispers kiss the night,
Carried soft on moonlit beams,
Each note a star, a flickering light,
In the fabric of our dreams.

A blanket of solace we share,
Knitted close by the threads of time,
In these echoes, we declare,
Comfort found in rhythm and rhyme.

## **A Lullaby of Sweet Whispers**

Underneath the silver moon,
Softly hums a gentle breeze,
Each note sings a tender tune,
While the world bends to its knees.

Whispers weave through the night air,
Cradling dreams in silken threads,
A lullaby that frees each care,
Guiding hearts to peaceful beds.

Stars twinkle in knowing grace,
They gather 'round, a celestial choir,
Embracing all in this warm space,
As hopes ignite the night's desire.

Feel the hush, let worries cease,
Breathe in rhythm, sweet release,
In these whispers, finding peace,
A lullaby that grants us ease.

## **Driftwood Dreams**

Along the shore where tides caress,
Driftwood stories drift along,
Each piece a memory to assess,
In nature's chorus, soft and strong.

The sea whispers secrets old,
Carried on the currents wide,
Every fragment, a tale retold,
In the ebb and flow, we confide.

Beneath the sun's warm, golden glow,
Dreams are scattered on the sand,
With every wave, they rise and flow,
A dance of hopes, both grand and planned.

Gather these dreams, let them weave,
A tapestry of calm and light,
In driftwood's grace, we believe,
Our hearts anchored through the night.

## **Celestial Comfort in Pause**

Stars twinkle softly in the night,
Whispers of dreams take their flight.
Moonbeams brush against the skin,
In this stillness, peace begins.

Breath of winds, a silent sigh,
Floating wonders gently lie.
In each heartbeat, time stands still,
Embracing calm, a quiet thrill.

## **Echoes of Peaceful Drowsiness**

Gentle breezes softly flow,
Crickets sing a lullaby low.
In this moment, minds will drift,
Wrapped in night's enchanted gift.

Clouds like pillows, dreams take shape,
In the dark, our spirits escape.
Swaying softly, hearts align,
In the hush, peace we find.

## Fables from the Sleepy Cosmos

Twilight tells of stories old,
In the stars, secrets unfold.
Galaxies spin their timeless yarns,
Painting dreams on velvet lawns.

Comets blaze in paths of light,
Guiding souls through the night.
Each constellation, a tale shared,
In the cosmos, all are spared.

## **Nestled in Fantasy's Fold**

In the arms of slumber's grace,
We find our dreams, a sacred space.
Woven tales of joy and hope,
In this realm, we learn to cope.

Fairy whispers, soft and sweet,
Dancing shadows, heart's retreat.
Nestled close, we drift away,
In fantasy, we long to stay.

## **Swaying in a Sleepy Breeze**

The leaves dance gently overhead,
Whispers of the wind softly spread.
A lullaby of nature's song,
In this haven, we belong.

The sun dips low, a golden hue,
With shadows deep, the world feels new.
In twilight's grasp, we find our peace,
As worries fade and calm increase.

Beneath the trees, we close our eyes,
Floating high in mellow skies.
The breeze, a friend, it wraps us tight,
In dreams, we drift through endless night.

In every sigh and gentle sway,
We find the magic of the day.
With hearts so light, we breathe and twirl,
In a sleepy dance, we greet the world.

## The Comfort of Daydreams

In soft-lit rooms where shadows play,
Thoughts of wonder drift away.
Colors blend in gentle hues,
Painting worlds we often choose.

A castle built of laughter bright,
Beneath the stars, our dreams take flight.
Waves that crash on shores of gold,
Tales of love and secrets told.

Each moment blooms in sweet delight,
Holding close the warmth of night.
In daydreams, life is rich and vast,
A place where future meets the past.

With every breath, we weave the thread,
Of visions swirling in our head.
A tender space where spirits soar,
In comfort, we find so much more.

## **Wandering Through Dreamscapes**

In twilight realms where shadows roam,
We wander far, we find our home.
Starlit paths and silver streams,
Chasing softly woven dreams.

Mountains tall with whispers clear,
Echoing wishes, drawing near.
In valleys deep with secrets kept,
Where silent hopes and laughter leapt.

Floating on a misty breeze,
We dance with fireflies, hearts at ease.
Through moonlit glades, we drift along,
To the rhythm of a tender song.

Each step unfolds a wondrous sight,
A tapestry of pure delight.
Wandering on through dreamscapes wide,
With every heartbeat, we abide.

## **Blankets Against the World**

Wrapped in warmth, we find our peace,
The outside noise begins to cease.
With blankets soft, a welcoming embrace,
We shelter here, our sacred space.

Outside, the storm may howl and rage,
But in our hearts, we're not a cage.
With whispered dreams and gentle sighs,
We soar like birds in painted skies.

Beneath the layers, fears dissolve,
In tender moments, we resolve.
With every stitch, a story spun,
Two souls united, we've just begun.

So let the world spin fast and free,
In our cocoon, it's you and me.
Together wrapped, we face the night,
With blankets strong, our spirits light.

## Embraced by the Gossamer Veil of Night

In twilight's grace, the shadows play,
Gentle whispers guide the way.
Stars awaken in the sky,
Cradling secrets, soft and shy.

Moonlight dances on the stream,
Casting dreams that softly gleam.
Veils of night, a tender shroud,
Echoes whisper, calm and loud.

The world surrenders to the night,
Wrapped in dreams, pure delight.
Embraced by magic, silent and bright,
We float on starlight, hearts in flight.

## Journey Through the Soft Clutches of Dreaming

In the realm where visions blend,
Every heartbeat, time does suspend.
Floats a whisper, soft and sweet,
Guiding souls on quiet feet.

Clouds of thought drift like the breeze,
Weaving tales through ancient trees.
Follow paths of shimmering light,
Cascading softly into night.

Here in dreams, we shed our fears,
Sailing softly through the years.
Embraced in whispers, we unite,
In the soft clutches of the night.

## **Whispers of a Soft Embrace**

In the stillness, words take flight,
Wrapped in warmth, the tender night.
Hearts entwined, we softly drift,
In whispers low, our spirits lift.

Like petals falling, sweet and slow,
Love's gentle touch, a soft glow.
Caressed by dreams, the world unseen,
In the whispers, we glean.

Embracing moments, fleeting and rare,
Bound together in silent prayer.
The softest sigh, a serene trace,
In the echoes of a warm embrace.

## **Starlit Sanctuary**

Beneath a sky adorned with light,
A sanctuary of pure delight.
Stars like lanterns, soft and clear,
Guard our dreams, hold us near.

In the stillness, hope awakens,
Within our hearts, the love unshaken.
Crickets sing a lullaby,
Underneath the vast, deep sky.

A haven where our spirits soar,
Finding peace and so much more.
In starlit corners, secrets dwell,
Creating magic, casting spells.

## Soothing Shadows of the Mind

In twilight's hush, soft whispers flow,
Where thoughts like rivers gently go.
A calming breeze through branches weaves,
In shadows deep, the spirit breathes.

Within the stillness, dreams take flight,
Each flutter whispers, 'Hold me tight.'
The weight of worries drifts away,
As stars embrace the end of day.

A tender light, a guiding glow,
Illuminates the paths we know.
In quiet corners, peace we find,
Soothing shadows of the mind.

The night unfolds, a silent gift,
In tranquil hours, spirits lift.
Embrace the dark, let worries rest,
Where soothing shadows feel the best.

## The Dreamweaver's Nook

Nestled in the folds of night,
A cozy space where visions light.
The Dreamweaver spins tales so sweet,
In a secret nook, where hearts can meet.

Whispers thread like silken lace,
Through a tapestry of time and space.
Each story blooms, a petal bright,
In the quiet realms of sleep's delight.

Stars align in a gentle swirl,
Creating worlds where wishes twirl.
In the nook where magic waits,
The Dreamweaver opens the gates.

With every sigh, the dreams unfold,
Softly wrapped in threads of gold.
In this haven, joy takes root,
In the Dreamweaver's sacred nook.

## Gentle Farewell to Today

As the sun sets with a fiery glow,
Soft shadows stretch, and breezes blow.
Whispers of evening softly call,
A gentle farewell as night starts to fall.

The sky painted in hues so warm,
Embraces the earth from the storm.
With every breathe, I release my cares,
Creating space for silent prayers.

Stars begin their twinkling dance,
In twilight's embrace, we find our chance.
To reflect on moments, laughter, and play,
As I bid a gentle farewell to today.

In the hush of night, peace prevails,
As dreams take flight on shimmering trails.
With every heartbeat, I find my way,
In the gentle farewell to this day.

## **Sighs of a Peaceful Heart**

In the quiet of a moonlit night,
A gentle sigh feels so right.
Each breath a mark of sweet release,
In the stillness, I find my peace.

Thoughts drift like clouds across the sky,
Carried softly, they flutter by.
In the garden of my tranquil thought,
Sighs of calm are quietly sought.

The world fades in a soft embrace,
Leaving behind its hurried race.
With every beat, my spirit starts,
To weave the sighs of a peaceful heart.

So here I linger, free and light,
In a canvas painted by the night.
With hopes that dance in serene art,
I cherish the sighs of a peaceful heart.

## Fuzzy Fluffs of Hope

In whispers soft, the clouds drift by,
Cotton dreams in the open sky.
A gentle touch, a warm embrace,
Hope floats lightly, setting the pace.

With every heartbeat, a wish takes flight,
Fuzzy fluffs dance in the gleaming light.
Beneath the sun's golden rays we stand,
Holding onto dreams, hand in hand.

Through fields of daisies, we skip and play,
Chasing shadows, where laughter stays.
Each moment cherished, a treasure rare,
Fuzzy fluffs of hope, lighter than air.

As twilight whispers, we close our eyes,
In the realm of dreams, hope never dies.
With every breath, let our spirits soar,
Fuzzy fluffs of hope forevermore.

## **Embracing the Midnight Breeze**

Under the stars, the night unfolds,
Embracing whispers, both soft and bold.
Cool air dances through leaves so bright,
A symphony plays in the hush of night.

Moonlight glimmers on the ocean's face,
Waves serenade with delicate grace.
With open arms, we invite the chill,
Embracing the midnight, our hearts can fill.

Secrets linger in the midnight hour,
Nature's beauty, an exquisite flower.
Every breeze tells a story untold,
Embracing the night, as dreams unfold.

Whispers of comfort surround our souls,
In the midnight breeze, we feel whole.
With every sigh, we breathe in the night,
Embracing the magic till morning's light.

## **Cradled by the Timeless**

In a world where moments softly blend,
Cradled by time, where beginnings end.
Memories whisper in shadows deep,
A timeless cradle where secrets sleep.

Gentle echoes of laughter ring,
In the heart of time, we dance and sing.
Through seasons changing, we find our way,
Cradled by timeless, day by day.

The sun will rise, and shadows will fall,
Yet in this cradle, we stand tall.
Time's embrace, a warm cocoon,
Cradled by love, we'll be safe soon.

With every heartbeat, a tale is spun,
Cradled by timeless, we are as one.
Through the fabric of days, we weave our dream,
Cradled by time, forever we'll gleam.

## **Luminescent Dreams**

In the silence of night, dreams softly gleam,
Painting the sky with a luminous beam.
Stars flicker gently, like thoughts set free,
In the tapestry of night, we find our key.

With each breath taken, magic unfolds,
Luminescent visions, precious as gold.
Floating on wishes, we sail the skies,
In the realm of dreams, where the heart flies.

Threads of light weave through the dark,
Igniting our spirits, a radiant spark.
With open hearts, we embrace the night,
Luminescent dreams, guiding our flight.

As dawn approaches, the dreams remain,
In the morning's light, we shed the pain.
Holding the glow of what once was real,
Luminescent dreams, forever we feel.

## **The Nest of Wishes**

In branches high, where dreams take flight,
A nest of hopes, in soft moonlight.
Each whisper cradled, tender and bright,
Yearning hearts hold, through the night.

With every sigh, a wish takes form,
Wrapping our souls, keeping us warm.
In silent prayers, together we swarm,
Threads of desire, a binding charm.

Nestled close, we weave our fate,
In woven dreams, we patiently wait.
As dawn breaks, love's gentle weight,
We find our future, intricate state.

Through the twilight, we learn and grow,
In this sacred space, our spirits flow.
A tapestry made, where heartbeats show,
In the nest of wishes, our dreams aglow.

## **Kisses from the Moonlight**

Silver beams dance on the ground,
Whispers of night, a gentle sound.
Each kiss from the moon, love profound,
In shadows deep, our hearts are found.

Bathed in glow, time stands still,
With every glance, my heart you fill.
In this embrace, all fears we kill,
As stars above, our wishes spill.

Beneath the arch of the night's embrace,
We find our magic, our special place.
In moonlit secrets, we trace,
The paths of dreams, with quiet grace.

Kisses that linger, moments divine,
Under the stars, forever you're mine.
In the magic of night, our souls align,
With kisses from the moon, our hearts entwine.

## Tucked Beneath the Infinite Sky

Beneath the stars, our dreams align,
In whispered wishes, hearts combine.
We chase the night, in love we shine,
Tucked beneath the sky, pure and fine.

Clouds drift slowly, shadows play,
Hand in hand, we wander, sway.
In the cool breeze, worries decay,
Under the endless, bright array.

The universe sings in quiet tones,
Where stardust waltzes, love atones.
In the warmth of night, our joy condones,
Crafting a world where no one moans.

Tucked beneath the vast expanse,
With every heartbeat, we take a chance.
In this embrace, we softly dance,
Together forever, in love's romance.

## **Dreams Woven in Stardust**

In twilight's glow, our visions soar,
Dreams like whispers, forever more.
Woven in stardust, our spirits pour,
Creating worlds that we explore.

Through shimmering light, our hopes ignite,
Casting shadows, dancing in sight.
Every heartbeat, a spark so bright,
In this canvas, love takes flight.

With laughter echoing in the night,
We write our stories, pure delight.
In constellations, futures write,
Through dreams woven, hearts unite.

In galaxies far, our wishes tread,
With stardust magic, paths we'll thread.
Together we dream, with love we're fed,
In the tapestry of life, forever led.

## Serene Adventures on the Pillow's Edge

On softest waves, dreams gently sway,
Whispers of night guide the way.
Stars twinkle bright like thoughts in flight,
Each moment cradles pure delight.

Drifting through tales with tender grace,
Time stands still in this sacred space.
A world unfolds, vast and free,
In shadows where the heart can see.

Through meadows lush, where laughter sings,
Magic in every dream that clings.
With every breath, the journey starts,
Adventures bloom in hopeful hearts.

Awake with dawn, yet still they play,
Memories linger from yesterday.
On pillow's edge, the dreams reside,
In peaceful realms, where souls abide.

### **Floating on Clouds of Blushing Twilight**

In hues of pink, the sky unfolds,
Secrets of dusk, in warmth, it holds.
Gentle breezes carry our sighs,
As stars peek out from velvet skies.

Floating softly on dreams we find,
Moments drift, leaving cares behind.
Whispers of twilight, sweet and near,
Embrace us close, we feel no fear.

Each heartbeat dances, each breath a song,
In this serene space, we belong.
Laughter wrapped in twilight's glow,
In the soft light, our spirits flow.

Together we chase the fading light,
Through clouds of love, we soar in flight.
Holding on tight, we taste the night,
Floating forever, our hearts alight.

## Wrapped in the Aroma of Morning Glories

Morning blooms in fragrant embrace,
Sunbeams kiss the earth's warm face.
Petals whisper secrets untold,
In every scent, a memory unfolds.

Softly the dew clings to each leaf,
Awakening dreams and quiet belief.
Birdsong ripples in gentle air,
A symphony played without a care.

The world in colors bursts anew,
With every glance, a stunning view.
Time slows down in this sacred place,
Each moment lingers, wrapped in grace.

Wrapped in the aroma, hearts ignite,
With morning glories, pure delight.
In nature's hand, we find our way,
Every sunrise, a brand new day.

## The Home of Night's Gentle Lull

In shadows deep, the night unfolds,
Tales of dreams the darkness holds.
Moonlight weaves a silver thread,
Guide us softly to our bed.

Whispers linger in the cool breeze,
Crickets sing among the trees.
The world exhales a soothing sigh,
As stars emerge in the quiet sky.

Each breath a promise, each thought a prayer,
In the home of night, we feel the care.
Wrapped in comfort, the heart finds peace,
In gentle lullabies, worries cease.

As dreams beckon, we close our eyes,
Embraced by night, a sweet surprise.
Together we'll wander through starry seas,
In the home of night, where our hearts find ease.

Milton Keynes UK
Ingram Content Group UK Ltd.
UKHW021127021124
450571UK00005B/74